The SUNNY Side of SELLING

SellingPower.

200 Side-Splitting Sales Cartoons

Book Design: Michael Aubrecht
Editor: Barbara Eilenfield
Print Production: Jeff Macharyas

The Sunny Side of Selling is published in the United States by
Personal Selling Power Inc., PO Box 5467, Fredericksburg, VA 22403
Telephone: 540/752-7000 • Web address: www.sellingpower.com

Printing: United Book Press
Library of Congress Preassigned Control Number: 2005909431

ISBN# 0-939613-43-3

The SUNNY Side of SELLING

SellingPower.

200 Side-Splitting Sales Cartoons

HoW To GET THE MoST fRoM THIS Book

1. Do not read this book while driving.
We don't want you to have your last laugh too soon.

2. Do not read this book while eating lunch.
You don't want to spray your food all over the table as a result of a spontaneous and spasmodic laugh attack.

3. Do not read this book before leaving for a business trip.
Your spouse may wonder why you're in such a great mood when you're about to leave.

4. Overuse of this book may turn you into a "laughaholic."
If that's the case, here is your three-step program:
First step: Log onto www.sellingpower.com.
Second step: Click on Daily Cartoon.
Third step: Get daily laugh fix.

We hope you enjoy *The Sunny Side of Selling*.
Everyone deserves a little sunshine.

Gerhard Gschwandtner
Founder and Publisher

P.S. Don't miss page 102. My favorite cartoon is on that page!

CONTENTS

1 APPOINTMENTS 9

2 PROSPECTING 17

3 SALES CALLS 29

4 SALES PROCESS 39

5 PRESENTATIONS 49

6 NEGOTIATION 57

7 CLOSING 63

8 PURCHASING 69

9 SALES MANAGEMENT 79

10 HIRING & FIRING 101

11 TRAINING 109

12 PSYCHOLOGY 115

13 ATTITUDE & MOTIVATION 123

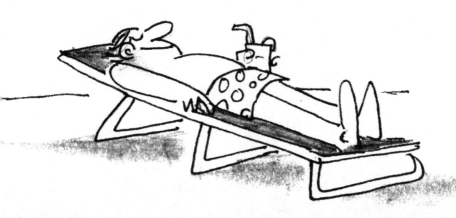

CHAPTER 1
APPOINTMENTS

No appointment necessary.
We heard you coming.

SIGN OUTSIDE MUFFLER SHOP

APPOINTMENTS

"Get pushy Shorty – I have salesmen like you for breakfast."

"When I said, 'I'll see you first thing in the morning,'
I meant in the office."

APPOINTMENTS

"No underlings please. I demand to see either a mover or a shaker."

"Thank you, Mr. Faraday, for squeezing in an appointment for me."

"Anything to the rumor that Mr. Tupan is resistant to salesmen?"

"Mr. Kelsey, that persistent salesman is here to see you again."

"Mr. Barston isn't seeing ANYONE today."

"So you're the receptionist. I wonder if salesmen
have a hard time getting past you?"

"You're early. Take a number."

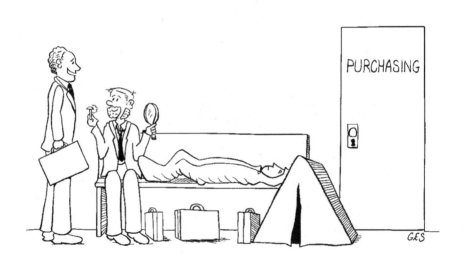

"Do we have to wait long?"

APPOINTMENTS

"Excuse me. Do you have an appointment?"

"He's not very receptive this morning."

CHAPTER 2

PROSPECTING

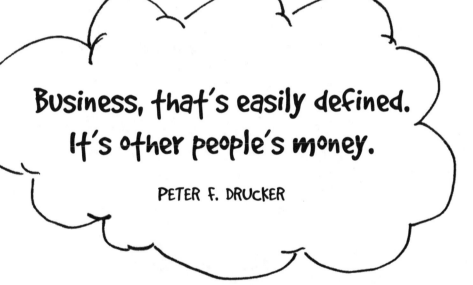

Business, that's easily defined. It's other people's money.

PETER F. DRUCKER

"Here's something that will improve your sales, Nerdly...
a briefcase with a snooze alarm."

"Whatever happened to that sales rep who used to follow you around?"

"It's the sales literature from ACME Missile. It's certainly designed to attract your attention."

"I'm making 'cold calls' today."

"Wow. He's got his timing down pat."

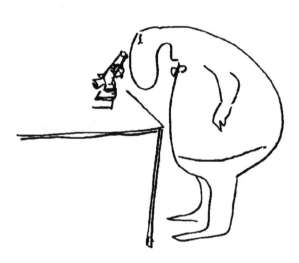

"All right Figgins! What's this about that territory being too small to make a living?"

"I'm tired of prospects who you consider a challenge.
Do you have one that's a cinch?"

"Snitkin, there really isn't any substitute for good ol' fashioned prospecting."

PROSPECTING

"If answering machines would place orders,
I'd be having a great month."

"Changed your mind yet about that policy?"

"I'm glad to see you're keeping your feelers out for potential business."

"Not that I'm complaining about the territory.
But I haven't sold one swimming pool."

"Why do I think you're using a script? Because frankly, I find it hard to believe that I was personally selected to try lingerie!"

"I'm working on a hot lead. He said he definitely was 'kinda – sorta' interested."

PROSPECTING

"I told you that going global would work. It's
a whole new customer base."

"Dad said if he was paying for the wedding, he's
entitled to a little something too."

"My sales manager says I'm not seeing as many prospects as I should."

"I go after a sales lead come hell or high water."

PROSPECTING

"Prospecting on empty."

"I'm not peeping. I'm prospecting."

CHAPTER 3

SALES CALLS

A bargain is something
you can't use at a price
you can't resist.

FRANKLIN JONES

"We're saved! I knew that as soon as I sent for that free
literature a salesman would show up."

"We already have a water softener. It's called 'summer.'"

SALES CALLS

"Okay, I'll buy a fire extinguisher. Boy, whoever supplies
your leads is really on the ball."

"This wouldn't happen again in a million years – you're one of my leads."

"Remember, push the corn."

"I didn't want one either, but the guy had such a great sales pitch."

"What good is studying the art of customers' hand gestures
when all you ever get is the thumbs-down?"

"Mr. Whitney says he's out, out, out, in and out."

"Look at the bright side of it... if a highway ever comes through, you won't mind giving it up."

"Pretty darn good salesman. You'd think she'd be the last person to order a pair of gloves."

SALES CALLS

"It sounds like a good deal – but I think I'll just shop around a bit."

"After I make my 'whole life spiel,' you stroll past his window."

SALES CALLS

"I don't know what it is, but that one always makes me nervous."

"Shall we go over your product item by item or would
you like to chicken out now?"

"Good morning, Mr. Jones. I'll be your salesman today. Assisting me will be Mr. Smith of Customer Service, Mr. Brown of Engineering, and Mr. Olsen of Merchandising."

"I think you should try some of my wife's cooking before you talk to me about life insurance."

CHAPTER 4

SALES PROCESS

I used to sell furniture
for a living. The trouble was,
it was my own.

LES DAWSON

"That's Johnson, he's our man in the field."

"They must have had a pretty advanced economy. It says,
'These sales lessons are also available on cassettes.'"

"I think I'll make a conference call."

"Could you change that objection, ma'am? My sales
manual doesn't contain a rebuttal for 'I hate you.'"

"I caught him by surprise. Nobody has ever tried to sell him 3 of anything."

"I bet you didn't expect me to sign the contract so soon, did you?"

SALES PROCESS

"Everybody's specializing these days."

"He wasn't very interested in our software, but
he might buy my old Buick."

"Son, take it from someone who's been selling for thirty years.
The best way to win over new clients is to buy them a meal."

"Just say we're reorganizing under Chapter 11, not
'we're going down the tube.'"

SALES PROCESS

"Marsha, why did we ever tell our sales manager
we were quick learners?"

"Since they put me on straight commission I've made a few sales.
I've sold my house, my car, my furniture..."

"We feel the play-by-play keeps what normally would
be tedious work a little more exciting."

"You didn't read the instructions – did you?"

SALES PROCESS

"What do you mean, I don't communicate?
Didn't you read the memo I left you at breakfast?"

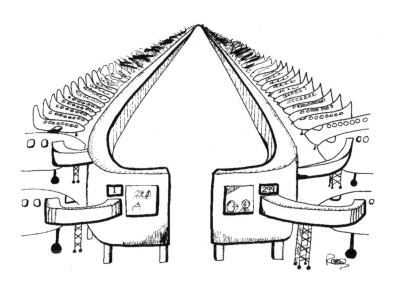

"Your connection leaves in five minutes from Gate 1."

CHAPTER 5

PRESENTATIONS

Nice to be here? At my age it's nice to be anywhere.

GEORGE BURNS

"Pretty clever way to sell fans. No one ever cuts her presentations short."

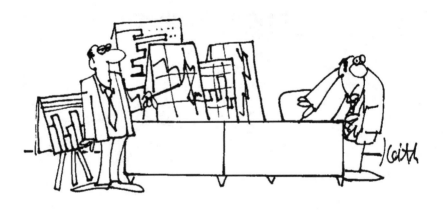

"This presentation is getting a little too graphic for me."

PRESENTATIONS

"This is the part that always gets to me – when they ask for the order."

"Let's face it. That's the ONE time we shouldn't have
tried to sell the sizzle or the steak."

"This is practically all the hardware you'll need to make our system compatible with any other."

"That sales rep unloads a lot of deodorizer. Apparently, he really knows how to create a demand for the product."

PRESENTATIONS

"I may buy from this sales team. Their body language looks impressive."

"We offer a wide variety of condominiums that come
in straw, twigs, or brick."

"So much for the interesting part. Now for the boring details."

"Yes, it's an excellent presentation, but that's no reason
to accuse him of taking steroids."

"It's a great program. You sell me your soul. Then you get five distributors to sell me their souls. Then each of them gets five distributors…"

"Do your sales presentation. That should get them to leave."

CHAPTER 6

NEGOTIATION

They say 'money can't buy love,' but it certainly improves your bargaining position.

CHRISTOPHER MARLOWE

"Is it a deal?"

"Quick! Call for backup!"

NEGOTIATION

"Why yes, this does mean that you get the order."

"No I don't think I'll sign yet. Your move."

"Checkmate."

"Give me three good reasons why you should get this order."

NEGOTIATION

"Next time I take out a group policy I'm looking at the small print."

"I am not high pressure, but now that you've bought the anchor,
how about a nice ocean liner to go with it?"

CHAPTER 7

CLOSING

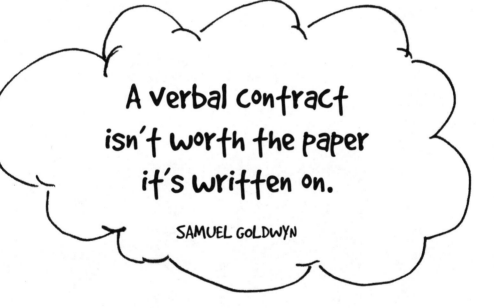

A verbal contract
isn't worth the paper
it's written on.

SAMUEL GOLDWYN

"Wait, you moron! Don't place a $50,000 order yet!
I haven't come to the close."

"This, I assume, is the close..."

CLOSING

"Must be a sales convention in town. They usually say, 'Repent!'"

"So you dropped by Murdock's Pet Shop. They say
he's quite an effective closer."

"Ms. Watkins adds the element of drama to our meetings that we find invaluable."

"Do you mind if I call my office for instructions? This is the first time I've gotten past the receptionist."

"With this particular account, use whatever trick you
have up your sleeve to close the deal."

"Let me close this deal first."

CHAPTER 8

PURCHASING

Fire the whole purchasing department. They'd hire Albert Einstein and then turn down his requisition for a blackboard.

ROBERT TOWNSEND

"Sir, the buyer will see you now."

"I wonder if it will work? After all, he's a salesman
and she's a purchasing agent."

"Their purchasing agent is a difficult man to see."

"I'm trying to decide on which long-distance service to use."

"As a matter of fact, I have just finished reviewing your price list."

"How can he possibly feel any job satisfaction as
a buyer, if he never buys anything?"

PURCHASING

"Take me to your buyer. I have come in peace."

"I gave him a good listening to."

"Don't be silly. I can't believe that a purchasing agent would deliberately try to intimidate a salesman."

"I want to buy your product, but I'm concerned about shipping costs."

"Purchasing has never been better. It's never been good,
so of course it's never been better."

"Our purchasing quota is simple. It ends with the words 'or else.'"

"I'm not sure if I want to purchase today. Tell you what, leave me your card and I'll get back to you."

"If you want to listen to music at work, purchase a WALKMAN!"

PURCHASING

"Why should I be sore? You won the game fair and square and now I don't feel any obligation to purchase anything from you."

"This may be harder than I thought."

CHAPTER 9

SALES MANAGEMENT

If you think your boss is stupid, remember; you wouldn't have a job if he was smarter.

ALBERT GRANT

SALES MANAGEMENT

"We're in agreement then, nobody knows what the hell these statistics mean."

"It's positively uncanny."

SALES MANAGEMENT

"Winston is here with the black box to see if we can figure out what went wrong last quarter."

"Quenton, do you think that's the appropriate attire for your first day as your firm's new general sales manager?"

SALES MANAGEMENT

"Relax Henson, you made your quota this month."

"Prophets are up."

SALES MANAGEMENT

"They're up to their old tricks again, making sure
everybody attends the staff meetings."

"Right there is when you decide to make our best
field salesmen District Managers."

"I don't know how you're doing it Clayton, but keep it up."

"I don't know where these salespeople get the
idea that I'm not accessible."

"He gets me so mixed up. First he tells me to use common sense in my sales approach, then he tells me to do it his way."

"We've driven our competition out of business. Now what do we do?"

"Yes, one of the reasons we've been so successful is
that our overhead is very low."

"What is it with you Hallawell? First your sales are up,
then down, then up, then down..."

SALES MANAGEMENT

"Remember that 'worst case scenario' we used to joke about?"

"Now you know why they call him 'reliable old Fred.'"

"I think we know who's at fault for this – don't we?"

Honesty in advertising – not always the best policy.

SALES MANAGEMENT

"I've heard several rumors that you're setting the
quotas too high – keep up the good work."

"Think, Benson – selling our product should be as easy as what?"

SALES MANAGEMENT

"He couldn't talk if you took the word 'quota' out of his vocabulary."

"Uh oh, I don't like the look of this."

SALES MANAGEMENT

"Every minute of every hour of every day someone out there
is making a sale – how come it isn't you?"

"You know what your problem is Jenkins? You've got a chip on your shoulder!"

"We've doubled our sales this month. Our two-for-one sale really worked."

"Oh no – the boss is in another one of his fowl moods."

"No Harris, you can't take sick leave just because
you don't feel positive today."

"Of course your ability to sell is improving a little, Benchly.
What else could it do?"

SALES MANAGEMENT

"So, I'm the world's worst sales manager – now isn't that a coincidence..."

"How about a merger?"

"He knows everything about our product except how to sell it."

"Benson, what's this business about you having
an extra mouth to feed now?"

SALES MANAGEMENT

"Don't tell me how rough things are out there, Simpson...
I've been there."

"That was the seventh employee to call in sick today,
it sounds like we all have a staff infection."

"Well I don't think it's very funny!"

"Miss Simpson, all of our salespeople are
in Las Vegas and Atlantic City again!"

"Sales are down 80%, but who cares?"

"Brewster, I think it's time we had a chat about your priorities."

SALES MANAGEMENT

"Very funny, wise guy! It's 'FORCE.'"

"Frankly, I was hoping our profits would have
been more obscene."

CHAPTER 10

HIRING & FIRING

If you've made it to thirty-five and your job still requires you to wear a name tag, you've made a serious vocational error.

DENNIS MILLER

"You are correct in that regard – we did advertise for someone
with 'street smarts,' Mr. Brandywine."

"Burton, if you're serious about helping out our company,
then go work for our competition."

"That's not exactly what I meant when I advertised
for a 'top salesman.'"

"What makes you think they're sending you to the hinterlands?"

"I think we can skip the polygraph exam Mr. Washington.
You have an honest face."

"Of course you're not fired. You're just under arrest."

"No one is doubting that you have a promising future,
but keep in mind, we're firing you for your past."

"I remember now – you were with the company
that always had the lowest price."

"Baxter, I really think you're wasting your time with a small firm like this. Why don't you try wasting your time with a bigger firm?"

"Don't think of it as a firing. Think of it as an exit-level position."

"What you'll need for me is an honest face when talking about the products and a straight face when talking about our prices."

"Let's put things in perspective here, Dunlo – you have delusions of grandeur... I actually have grandeur."

CHAPTER 11

TRAINING

Pair off in threes.
YOGI BERRA
at Spring Training

"I want to apologize for the delay. It seems our speaker has yet to arrive."

"Everybody leaving reminds me of another funny story."

TRAINING

"Does anybody have any questions?"

"I realize some of us here are in competition, but if
we could just put that aside for the moment..."

"The meek will not inherit the world – the assertive will sell it to them."

"Wake up! This is important!"

TRAINING

"I'd say thrill seekers or another executive adventure training seminar."

"Who came first – the buyer or the seller?"

CHAPTER 12

PSYCHOLOGY

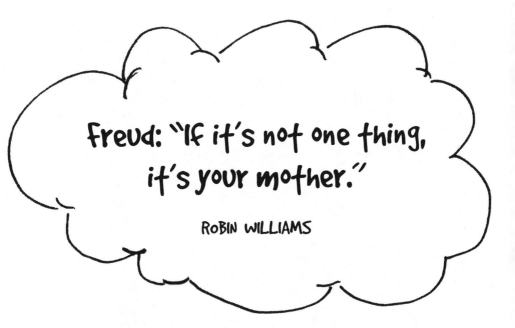

freud: "If it's not one thing,
it's your mother."

ROBIN WILLIAMS

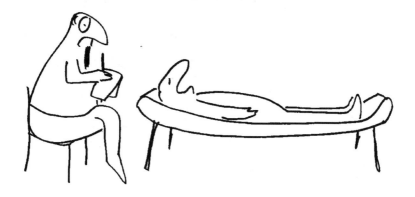

"Well Doc, I decided I needed help when I discovered my multiple personalities were holding conference calls."

"Now just sit back and relax and forget about business."

"I'm a sales guru. The regular guru is two mountains over."

"Typical salesman's hand. Your lifeline is fine. It's your bottom line you have to worry about."

"I wanted a big desk to make me feel like I've earned this position, but now that I've got it I feel small and insignificant."

"According to my manager, I'm still trying to find myself."

"No ulcers, nervous tics or high blood pressure.
You haven't been in sales long have you?"

"The word is that Hones isn't considered much of a team player."

"Your career seems to have plateaued."

"You say as a salesman, you believe everyone is against you.
Well, we're making progress – you're right!"

PSYCHOLOGY

"I almost went in there once."

"As usual, Simpson – you're trying to skirt the issue."

CHAPTER 13

ATTITUDE & MOTIVATION

I always arrive late
at the office, but I make up
for it by leaving early.

CHARLES LAMB

"Jones, I don't know what you did last Monday, but DON'T DO IT AGAIN!"

"Here's a one-way ticket. Land the order and I'll wire you the return fare."

"We all make mistakes; just don't let this one destroy the confidence you'll need to find another job."

"He's in motivational research."

"I might be Bob Smith to you, but on the phone I'm Pavarotti."

"Spare some change?"

"Money talks, but it's never spoken my language."

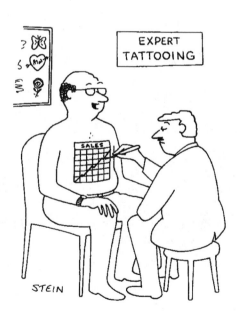

"...and I doubt if I'll ever see another year like it."

"Miss Lindvall, be careful who you lend my motivation tapes to."

"This new car is remarkably easy to peddle.
Why, I've sold six in just one day!"

"The only order I got today was, 'Get out and stay out.'"

"I see you made this month's issue."

"You're lucky you got out with the first downsizing."

"You have a very warped sense of humor."

"This is good stuff."

"One more sale this month and more greatness will be thrust upon me."

"No offense Miss Winthrop, but have you ever considered writing a book on salesmanship?"

"Yes Peters, I like ambition. Now get the hell out from behind my desk!"

"If you don't feel exploited, you're not working hard enough."

"Maybe I'll sell that Clayton account after all."

ACKNOWLEDGMENTS

For many years, *Selling Power* offered readers a look at the lighter side of sales. Cartoonists from all over America submitted their 'toons, created in such varied locations as a rough lean-to in the deep woods of the remote northwest to a jailhouse in the northeast. Cartoonists in cities and on farms, in the Florida Keys and in the center of Kansas put pen to paper to make readers laugh out loud.

In this collection, *Selling Power* editors have selected a broad range of cartoons covering major phases of the selling cycle. Or should we say, the silly cycle. To the list of cartoonists below the editors and readers offer thanks for the laughs.

Masters Agency	Al Kaufman	H.L. Schwadron
Charles Almon	Keith Larson	John R. Shanks
Gordon M. Bartlett	Sam Lloyd	Mike Shapiro
Wm. H. Boserman	Gene Machamer	Bill Shelly
Brenda A. Brown	A.A. McCourt	Goddard Sherman
Francis H. Brummer	Theresa McCracken	Stewart Slocum
Dave Carpenter	Dale McFeathers	Gary E. Smith
Sandy Dean	Bill Mittlebeeler	Eli Stein
James Estes	Bill Murray	Richard Stubler
George Hartman	Harry Nelson	Frank Tabor
Lowell Hoppes	John T. Paine	Andrew Toos
Cartoons By Johns	Jesse L. Rezendes	Arthur Winburg
Cliff Johnson	Tony Saltzman	Mike Woodruff
John E. Karp	Bob Schochet	